P9-CQN-061

Great Explorers

Jacques Cousteau

by Jim Ollhoff

Visit us at
www.abdopublishing.com

Published by ABDO Publishing Company, PO Box 398166, Minneapolis, MN 55439.
Copyright ©2014 by Abdo Consulting Group, Inc. International copyrights reserved in all countries. No part of this book may be reproduced in any form without written permission from the publisher. ABDO & Daughters™ is a trademark and logo of ABDO Publishing Company.

Printed in the United States of America, North Mankato, Minnesota
052013
012014

 PRINTED ON RECYCLED PAPER

Editor: John Hamilton
Graphic Design: Sue Hamilton
Cover Design: Neil Klinepier
Cover Photo: Corbis
Interior Photos & Illustrations: ABC via Getty Images-pgs 17 & 25; Alamy-pg 22; AP-pgs 7, 9, 20, 27 & 29; Corbis-pgs 19, 21 & 24; Courtesy MIT Museum-pg 12; Getty-pgs 10, 11, 13, 15 & 26; Granger-pgs 6 & 31; iStockphoto-compass illustration; NASA-pg 4; National Geographic-pg 23; Thinkstock-pgs 5, 8, 18 & grunge map background illustration.

ABDO Booklinks
To learn more about Great Explorers, visit ABDO Publishing Company online. Web sites about Great Explorers are featured on our Book Links pages. These links are routinely monitored and updated to provide the most current information available. Web site: www.abdopublishing.com

Library of Congress Control Number: 2013931665

Cataloging-in-Publication Data

Ollhoff, Jim.
Jacques Cousteau / Jim Ollhoff.
   p. cm. -- (Great explorers)
ISBN 978-1-61783-966-5
1. Cousteau, Jacques, 1910-1997--Juvenile literature. 2. Oceanographers--France--Biography--Juvenile literature. I. Title.
551.46/092--dc23
[B]   2013931665

Contents

Early Ocean Exploration

About 71 percent of the world's surface is covered in water. The oceans are all connected, which gives boats access to much of the world. Many goods are transported across the ocean, and many products, such as sea salt and fish, come from the sea. The oceans support many industries, and provide tourism and recreational opportunities. In fact, more than 15 percent of jobs in North America are somehow related to the ocean, and over one-third of all people live within 60 miles (97 km) of an oceanic coast.

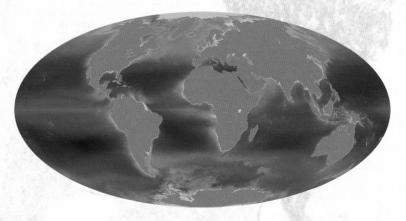

Left: Oceans cover about 71 percent of Earth's surface. People worldwide rely on the oceans to provide work, food, and enjoyment.

Above: Half of all of Earth's species live in the world's seas and oceans. Jacques Cousteau said, "The sea, once it casts its spell, holds one in its net of wonder forever."

Oceans greatly influence the weather and climate of our planet. The world's seas and oceans support nearly half of all species on Earth. Many of the medicines we use come from ocean plants. The world's oceans are a vital part of the environment and human life.

People have been sailing the oceans since before civilization began. They explored the world on boats, colonized new areas, and traded with others over the oceans. The oceans provided food for the earliest civilizations, and still provide us with much food today.

Even though oceans are critical to our survival, not very much was known about the underwater world until recently. Scientists were slow to study the ocean depths, largely because the technology wasn't available to travel deeply underwater.

Above: An Egyptian merchant ship illustrated on a tomb. Egyptians tried to measure the depth of the Mediterranean Sea using poles and sinkers.

As early as 1800 BC, the Egyptians tried to measure the depth of the Mediterranean Sea using poles and sinkers. The Greek philosopher Aristotle (384–322 BC) was one of the first people to study the sea. He took measurements of the tides, and he started to catalog sea animals. He also figured out that evaporation and rain were part of the same process, because the oceans never dried up.

In the 1500s, Spanish and Portuguese sailors began to understand ocean currents. These "rivers" of water that run through the oceans enabled Christopher Columbus, and those who followed him, to sail to and from North and South America faster and more reliably.

Captain James Cook (1728–1779) explored and mapped many parts of the Pacific Ocean. He brought along scientists and naturalists so that more could be learned about the oceans.

Matthew Fontaine Maury (1806–1873) was the superintendent of the United States Naval Observatory from 1842–1861. He produced the first textbook on oceanography.

Even with advances in oceanography, by the early 1900s there were still many questions about what was under the water. Few people knew what lay in the depths of the oceans. It has often been said, half-jokingly, that in the mid-1900s we knew more about the moon than we did about the ocean.

And then along came Jacques Cousteau, one of the greatest underwater explorers that ever lived. Thanks to this soft-spoken Frenchman, our knowledge of the world's oceans increased like never before. Often seen with his familiar red cap, he was a passionate advocate for the oceans and marine life.

Left: Underwater explorer Jacques Cousteau wears his familiar red cap. Cousteau said, "The future is in the hands of those who explore… and from all the beauty they discover while crossing perpetually receding frontiers, they develop for nature and for humankind an infinite love.

Jacques Cousteau: Early Years

Jacques Cousteau was born on June 11, 1910, in the city of Saint-André-de-Cubzac in France. As a young child, he was often sick, and doctors said he should not do any vigorous activity. Despite their advice, he learned to swim. He especially loved swimming in the ocean. He did not do well in school, but he was curious about mechanical objects, especially film cameras.

Right: A swimmer dives into the ocean. Jacques Cousteau loved swimming in the ocean in his youth. His friends nicknamed him "the manfish."

Cousteau attended college in Paris. In 1930 he entered the French Naval Academy. He graduated in 1933 and then entered the French navy. He was training to become a pilot when a bad automobile accident nearly killed him. No longer qualified for flight training and needing time to heal, he went back to his first love: the ocean. In 1936, he got a pair of goggles that could be worn underwater. Being able to see beneath the water fired his curiosity even more. He was so comfortable swimming in the ocean that friends called him "the manfish."

Cousteau married Simone Mechior in 1937. Simone shared her husband's passion for exploring the seas. Together they had two sons, Jean-Michel and Phillipe. Both of them later in life would follow in their father's footsteps and become explorers and advocates for the ocean.

Above: Jacques Cousteau, his wife, Simone, and their pet dachshund aboard their ship, *Calypso*, in 1950.

The Aqua-Lung

Cousteau enjoyed swimming, but wanted to explore underneath the water for longer periods, instead of coming up for air every minute or two. He began to wonder, "Is there a way that people might breathe underwater?"

There had been diving suits in use under the water. They had a metal helmet, heavy shoes, and a suit connected with air hoses to a ship on the surface. People on the ship would pump air down the hose so that the diver could breathe. The suit was heavy and bulky, and the diver couldn't swim. The diver had to walk, and hope that the air hose didn't get twisted or tangled. The people on the ship had to haul the diver up when the work was done.

Right: A 1915 Navy crew prepares to send a diver down. At the time, divers wore heavy metal helmets with air hoses connected to a pump on the surface.

Jacques Cousteau (right)
prepares to dive using an
early version of the Aqua-Lung.

Above: In 1953, Jacques Cousteau and engineer Emile Gagnan discuss the design of a new version of an Aqua-Lung.

Cousteau wanted to be able to swim, not walk, underwater. He wanted the freedom to go anywhere while he was underwater, and not be attached to a surface ship. He worked with an engineer named Emile Gagnan to develop a way to breathe underwater.

In 1943, the pair invented the Aqua-Lung. This was an apparatus made of two air tanks strapped to a diver's back. A device called a regulator allowed the right amount of air to come out of the tanks. The diver breathed the air through a mouthpiece. The Aqua-Lung allowed divers to swim and breathe for long periods underwater. It became known as the Self-Contained Underwater Breathing Apparatus, or SCUBA.

Above: A U.S. Navy diver works underwater using scuba gear in 1951.

In the French Navy

In 1939, World War II began. The United States, England, the Soviet Union, and other allies were at war with Nazi Germany, Japan, and Italy. Cousteau was trained as a gunnery officer, but he also joined the French navy's information service. After France fell to the Nazis in 1940, Cousteau moved his family to the town of Megeve, France, near the border of Switzerland. After that, he spied on Italian troop movements. He passed information to the French Resistance, a network of groups that fought the German soldiers.

Even during the war, Cousteau continued his mission to explore the ocean. He built a camera that could work underwater without being damaged by the water or the pressure. Even with his duties in the navy, he made two film documentaries about undersea exploration.

Cousteau received several medals for his work with the Resistance, including the prestigious Legion of Honor. After the war, he worked with the French navy and ships called minesweepers. He worked to clear underwater bombs, called mines, that were left over from the war.

Opposite Page:
In 1943, Jacques Cousteau directed and narrated his second underwater film named *Épaves* (*Wrecks*). This was the first film to feature the Aqua-Lung diving system.

JEAN COLIN

FRÉDÉRIC DUMAS
PH. TAILLIEZ
DANS

épaves

UN FILM DE
JACQUES-YVES COUSTEAU
MUSIQUE DE PIERRE CAPDEVIELLE

The Undersea World of Jacques Cousteau

Above: A poster for Jacques Cousteau's 1956 Academy Award-winning documentary, *The Silent World.*

In 1950, Cousteau obtained an old minesweeper and retooled it as a research and exploration vessel. Its name was *Calypso.* Cousteau was becoming increasingly concerned about humanity's impact on the ocean. Pollution, overfishing, and garbage dumping were damaging the Earth's oceans. He wanted to show people how beautiful the ocean was, but also wanted to make people aware of how they were harming the underwater world.

Cousteau began to write books and make documentaries. Two of his films, *The Silent World* (1956) and *World Without Sun* (1964), won Academy Awards for best documentaries.

Above: In 1970, Jacques Cousteau prepares to dive during the filming of his television show, *The Undersea World of Jacques Cousteau.*

Above: A sea turtle swims past a school of fish. Jacques Cousteau brought the beauty of the oceans to millions of people in his TV series *The Undersea World of Jacques Cousteau.*

Cousteau worked on many projects. He became the director of the Oceanographic Museum of Monaco, founded research groups, and headed the Conshelf program, an experiment in underwater living. He arranged for the exploration of sunken ships.

In 1966, Cousteau starred in an hour-long television special called *The World of Jacques-Yves Cousteau.* This exposed millions of people to the beauty and mystery of the oceans. Beginning in 1968, he produced the TV series *The Undersea World of Jacques Cousteau.* This show made Cousteau very famous worldwide. The show lasted for nine seasons. He highlighted undersea places all over the world and described marine life. He showed up-close images of whales, dolphins, coral reefs, and all kinds of animals and plants living in the ocean. In his ship, *Calypso,* he highlighted how human activity was damaging the oceans and marine life.

Left: Jacques Cousteau stands with his Society of Camera Operators Lifetime Achievement Award in September 1995. It was one of many awards given to the great explorer during his life.

Cousteau continued his work in many areas: fund-raising, writing books, making speeches, and managing the museum in Monaco. He was also involved in political action and conservation efforts.

Cousteau was awarded many honors throughout his life, including the 1961 National Geographic Gold Medal. In 1985 he was awarded the Presidential Medal of Freedom by President Ronald Reagan.

Jacques Cousteau: Final Years & Continued Exploration

Below: In 1996, Cousteau's *Calypso* was struck by a barge and sank while in the port of Singapore.

Cousteau's wife, Simone, died in 1990. He later married Francine Triplet. Cousteau and Francine had a son and daughter.

In January 1996, Cousteau's research vessel *Calypso* accidentally collided with a barge and sank. As Cousteau was trying to raise money to build a new vessel, he died of heart failure on June 25, 1997. He was 87 years old. He died in Paris, France, and was buried in the city of his birth.

Left: Jacques Cousteau waves from the deck of a ship. The French undersea explorer founded the Cousteau Society in 1973. It exists today with more than 50,000 members. The Cousteau Society states its mission as: "Educating people to understand, to love and to protect the water systems of the planet, marine and fresh water, for the well-being of future generations."

In 1973, Jacques Cousteau founded the Cousteau Society. This organization still exists today, and is dedicated to marine exploration and protecting the oceans for future generations. It boasts tens of thousands of members from all over the world. After Cousteau's death, his wife Francine took over leadership of the Cousteau Society.

Cousteau's son Jean-Michel formed his own oceanographic organization called the Ocean Futures Society. Jacques Cousteau's granddaughter, Alexandra, created an organization called Blue Legacy to advocate for water issues. Other members of the Cousteau family are involved in ocean exploration and conservation as well.

The Cousteau Society continues to carry out its founder's goals: to educate people about the ocean's fragile ecosystems, and to be a voice for the protection of the oceans. Cousteau believed that only educated people could make good decisions about how to protect the oceans. With an extensive book collection and more than 100 films, the Cousteau Society shares ocean explorations from Antarctica to northern Canada. The Society has also developed many educational curriculums for students of all ages.

Below: Alexandra Cousteau, granddaughter of Jacques Cousteau, heads Blue Legacy. She and her organization encourage the conservation and protection of water resources in order to maintain a healthy planet.

The Cousteau Society continues to work with scientists on projects, from developing better technology for seeing underwater life to more eco-friendly ways of ship transportation. The Society works with scientists to measure nutrients in the ocean and gauge progress in reducing damage from pollution. It also works with governments to protect whales, reefs, and other marine habitats.

Cousteau's Legacy

Below: A diver observes a spider crab. Through books, films, and television, Jacques Cousteau brought the beauty of the oceans to millions of people.

Jacques Cousteau was a showman and an educator. At a time when the oceans were an unknown mystery, he unveiled the beauty of the deep. He showed people what was underneath the water. He lived and worked at a time when people routinely dumped garbage into the ocean. Governments often dumped toxic or radioactive waste into the water. People thought the waste would just "go away." Cousteau showed how that practice damaged marine life. He showed, up close and personal, that ocean life was fragile. Cousteau became a passionate voice for the protection of oceans.

His television show, *The Undersea World of Jacques Cousteau*, made exploration popular. Prior to Cousteau, few people had seen anything below the surface of the water. Through his books, films, and his decades of ocean exploration, he showed images and video that made lasting impressions on millions of people.

Above: Jacques Cousteau prepares for an episode of his TV show, *The Undersea World of Jacques Cousteau*.

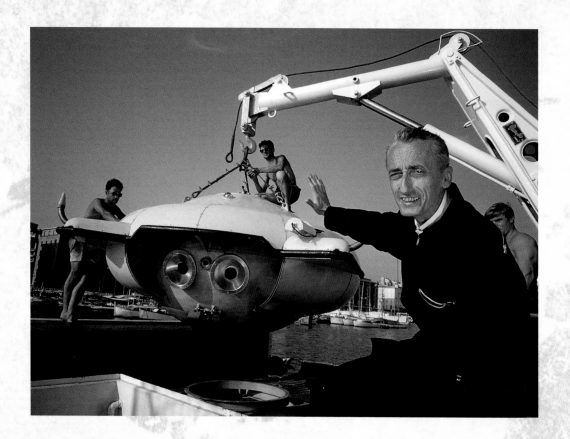

Above: Jacques Cousteau gestures toward the first underwater vessel designed specifically for scientific research. The two-person diving saucer was built in 1959. It could dive to a depth of 1,148 feet (350 meters).

Cousteau was also an inventor. With help from others, he built the Aqua-Lung. He continued to improve on the device in future years. He designed underwater film cameras. He helped create small submarines that could ferry divers back and forth. He designed undersea houses where "aquanauts" could work for days or weeks at a time.

Cousteau's influence caused some big environmental successes. In 1960, the French government planned to dump toxic radioactive waste into the Mediterranean Sea. He came out against it, and got others involved in the process. The train carrying the toxic waste had to stop when protestors sat on the railroad tracks.

Prior to Cousteau, many nations hunted whales. As whale populations dwindled, Cousteau began to speak out against the practice. He was able to secure laws in many countries against whaling.

In 1972, Cousteau visited Antarctica. His film, *Voyage to the Edge of the World*, helped show the beauty and fragility of the ice continent. He launched a worldwide effort to protect the pristine lands of Antarctica. In the late 1970s, many countries wanted to look for precious minerals or oil there. Mining operations and oil drilling would have severely damaged the Antarctic environment. Cousteau's efforts helped to stop exploitation.

Above: Jacques Cousteau poses in front of a life-size blue whale replica in front of Paris's Arc de Triomphe (Arch of Triumph). The blue whale was displayed in a marine museum. Cousteau was an avid protector of whales.

Timeline

1910, June 11	Jacques Cousteau is born in France.
1930	Cousteau enters the French Naval Academy.
1933	Cousteau enters the French Navy.
1936	Receives his first pair of underwater goggles.
1937	Marries Simone Mechior.
1940	Begins to work for the French Resistance in World War II.
1943	With Emile Gagnan, develops the underwater breathing apparatus called the Aqua-Lung.
1950	Retools an old British navy minesweeper as a research and exploration vessel. It is called *Calypso*.
1956 & 1964	Wins Academy Awards for best documentaries for his films *The Silent World* (1956) and *World Without Sun* (1964).
1966	Stars in an hour-long TV special *The World of Jacques-Yves Cousteau*.
1968	Begins production of the TV series *The Undersea World of Jacques Cousteau*.
1973	Creates the Cousteau Society.
1991	Marries Francine Triplet.
1997, June 25	Cousteau dies in Paris, France.

Above: Jacques Cousteau stands on the deck of his refurbished vessel *Calypso* in 1986.

Glossary

Aqua-Lung

An apparatus allowing divers to breathe air from tanks strapped to their backs. Its invention in 1943 lets divers spend long periods of time underwater.

Calypso

The famous vessel that traveled all over the world conducting research and carrying Jacques Cousteau as he filmed his documentaries.

Cousteau Society

An organization, started by Jacques Cousteau, that educates and advocates for marine ecosystems and the oceans.

French Resistance

Networks of French citizens during World War II that fought back against the German occupation of France.

Oceanography

The scientific study of the oceans.

Regulator

A device that allows a diver to breathe from a scuba tank. Because compressed air inside a scuba tank is at extremely high pressure, the regulator is needed to "regulate" the pressure and allow the diver to breathe safely.

SCUBA

Equipment that allows divers to breathe underwater without a hose attached to the surface or other air supply. SCUBA stands for Self-Contained Underwater Breathing Apparatus.

Above: Jacques Cousteau was famous for his iconic red knit watch cap. It was commonly worn by sailors and divers to stay warm.

Index